WHAT UNEMPLOYED?

WHAT
UNEMPLOYED?

DIANA LEFF

REINVENT YOURSELF

Plan A: You have the gift of life, so reinvent yourself, and do something different.

WHAT CAN YOU DO RIGHT NOW?

Make a list of all the things you know you can do, such as mow the lawn, and so on, to make additional money for your family, friends, and pets that you are responsible for.

✓ Can you garden?

✓ Can you paint? Pictures, walls.

WHAT IS IT THAT YOU KNOW HOW TO DO?

Even if you would never use it as a career, it is something that you can do. This is like taking a picture of yourself: what your life is like and what it can be like if you go back to school. You are never too old to learn.

OTHER IDEAS

Move to a farm. There are many different kinds of farms.

Do your résumé or redo your résumé. See if you can change any of it, make it look different. Make different résumés for different employers. They are all looking for different things and strengths.

Sometimes you apply for one position, and then they say, "We gave that position to another candidate, but we have another position in another department. Would you be interested in interviewing for that department?"

✓ Say yes. You will talk to the other manager.

✓ Find out if there are openings in your field.

✓ Can you get into another field?

Can you find a different job that you can do without additional education, or do you need to go back to school because you want to go to a different field?

EVEN MORE IDEAS

Do you know how to cook? Can you cook for others and get paid?

A man I know never went to school. He was raised on the family farm, and he always cooked for his family. One morning he put a large barbecue in front of the farm where the streets were, and he started to cook some ribs with his sauce that everyone loved. Early in the morning, everyone going by saw the man cooking, and they could smell those delicious ribs with that sauce.

There was a sign he had his friend write: "Please come taste my ribs. They are delicious." At lunch so many people came that all the ribs were gone in an hour, so the next day he doubled the amount of meat he brought, and it was gone in an hour. Double the number of people had come to taste his ribs. He never left the farm because everyone loved his ribs.

QUESTIONS TO ASK YOURSELF

✓ What do you know?

✓ Whom do you know?

✓ What do you have?

✓ Do you have a car?

✓ Do you have a car payment?

✓ When will you be done paying for the car?

✓ Will it be good enough for a few years so that you can put some money away, or are you going to need another car soon?

THINGS TO DO: UNEMPLOYMENT BENEFITS

The first thing you must do is apply for unemployment benefits to see if you qualify. Many people qualify. If you do not enter your résumé with the unemployment office, they will not send you your check. For example, it must be entered at edd.ca.gov if you live in California.

All information must be included. If you forget the zip code, they will reject your claim, and you will have to start from the beginning.

And if for any reason you do not qualify, find out why. Maybe there is a reason you don't know about that is keeping them from qualifying you. But even if you don't qualify, it's OK. You can go to plan B.

YOUR RÉSUMÉ

Then do your résumé, and enter it on all employment and recruiting websites that you know of, so different employers can see your résumé. This includes the Employment Development Department (EDD) website. Maybe an employer will call you.

EDD

✓ Did the EDD qualify you for any amount, or did they reject you because you were self-employed?

✓ What will your income be now that you have lost your job?

✓ Do you have any income now?

QUESTIONS TO ASK YOURSELF

✓ Do you own any property?

✓ What are your assets?

✓ What are your debts?

✓ What debts can you pay off now? Or what can you not get out of because you cannot afford it?

✓ Did you just buy a car on credit the month before you got fired, quit, or left your company by resigning?

✓ Create a budget for your new income, whatever that may be.

✓ Do you have savings that you can get your hands on? If you do, how much longer will you last with the money you have?

UNEMPLOYMENT

Maybe for a few days or years, you will have great difficulty finding a new job in the same field or a different field. Look and see what is available in your area and then expand to other areas.

If you are still finding it difficult, then look in other states and countries if you have your BA or better.

If you do not have your college degree, you can still apply for jobs in other countries, but it will be harder for the other countries to OK your forms for the right to work in the other countries.

EMPLOYERS

All employers look online for employees. They want the best candidates for their companies. They want the best that they can find.

Many companies have their own websites that you can apply through. You can apply at their company and add your résumé in their files so if there is another position available, they will see your résumé first through the company's website.

INVENTORY

Do an inventory of all the things you have. What can you sell, if anything?

For how many years can you keep these things you have and use?

List the things that you will need this year and next year. Think about your family and pets. List all the things you will need in the next year for you and your family and your pets. What things do you have? Remember things like oil changes for your car.

It is expensive to have pets. They need your love, food, and water. They also need medical attention yearly.

There are no job advertisements in newspapers. They are all on-line. Everything is done with a computer.

WHAT ARE YOUR EXPENSES?

An expense is money that is going out. What habits must you change due to your unemployment? These may be changes just for now.

✓ What will your new income be, if any? Can you live on it?

✓ Do you have a 401(k)? This is an emergency. Look at it. Can you take money out?

✓ How much money is in that account, if any?

KEEP TRYING!

Don't sit and wait for employers to call you because most of the time, they will not call, and if they do, it will be only once.

Find new places to send your resume everyday.

Talk to friends and family, an inside track is the best way to get an interview!

EDUCATION

✓ Can you go back to school? Maybe you can.

✓ Maybe you think you cannot go back to school?

Now in Los Angeles our government is starting a program for people that never went to college, and you can go for free or almost for free if you go full time.

DEBT

✓ How much debt do you have? Family debt? House debt? Car debt?

✓ How many children do you have?

✓ What will your needs be?

Will you have help from family and maybe friends? Coworkers are not your friends. When you leave that company, they will not call you. They do not care. It is not them, it's you. And they still have their jobs.

Not until you have been working for many years and have many special coworkers will one or two of them still call you a friend. But it is very rare that they will call you.

INSURANCE

If you have insurance, that is great. For how long will the insurance last? A month or a year?

If you do not have insurance, there are many clinics in every city that you can go to and hospitals that have payment plans for the uninsured. The best idea is to go to clinics unless it is a medical emergency. Then go to the nearest hospital. You will figure things out later.

That is why you should go to your nearest hospital and ask them what plans they have for the uninsured. That way if something happens, you will know what to do.

You need to know what to do if something happens to your loved ones or you from the stress of unemployment. And if something happens to you and you have not started collecting unemployment, you can get disability. I do not think that you will qualify if you have no benefits.

If you get in a car accident, then your car insurance will pay if you have full coverage.

PRAY

It is a good thing to pray if you can. Prayer is the best thing. Ask and you will receive. Look and you will find.

God loves you whether you pray to him or not. He just loves you.

CONTRACT ASSIGNMENT

This just means the job is a contract for a day or a week or a month, maybe five months, but it is not permanent. This means that you could lose your job for any reason. And also, if you do not like the temporary assignment, you could stop going for any reason.

It does not matter if the employer says, "The assignment is for one week," because if they need you, they could keep you for a year. The temporary agency will give you medical, dental, and vacation too. After the first week, you will get a paycheck.

Many times I was told that the assignment was for one week, and then I would work for five or six months as a temp with all my benefits and vacation time too. When my assignment was over, I reapplied for unemployment benefits.

UNEMPLOYMENT BENEFITS

You have become unemployed, and therefore you may qualify for benefits. Now, if a week after, you fall and break your leg, you must call and tell them that you cannot look for work with your broken leg. And then you should apply for disability payments.

Disability means that you are ill, are sick, had surgery, or similar. Your doctor must sign the disability papers from the disability department.

Once you are well again and OK'd by your doctor, then you can apply for unemployment benefits again.

Disability checks are much larger than unemployment checks, but you'll get what you qualify for.

If you cannot work, the EDD will not pay you until you can work.

And you should see if you qualify again.

Unemployment checks are time sensitive.

STRESS

Stress can be terrible on the body. Therefore, take care of yourself. It is not good to be unemployed and sick and tired and in pain.

Try to stay healthy and clean, and eat right if you can.

HOMELESSNESS

Do not think that because you have a great job today that you will not be unemployed tomorrow. Many great people have been unemployed and lost everything. That is why you must save for a rainy day.

Remember that if it does not rain, the seed cannot open up so that the flower will come out and see the sun.

COMPANIES

Many companies are creating machines that will enable them to have fewer employees.

These machines will break down, and they will need to be fixed.

NOTE

This is a great opportunity for you to do something different whether you would like to or not.

NEED TO DO

Whether you have worked for six months or thirty years, you need to apply for unemployment benefits as soon as you become unemployed to see if you can get benefits.

It will take some time. Then the EDD will get back to you with the news about whether you have benefits. Once you receive that letter, they will start sending you your benefit checks.

If you do not apply and wait until you are broke, your benefit time may be up, and you may miss out on the thousands of dollars that you would have received. You will not receive this money because your time is up. And the EDD is no longer working on those months.

EXCUSES

✗ I do not have time.

✗ I do not speak English well.

✗ I do not know how to talk on the phone.

✗ I do not know how to use a computer.

✗ I had a fight with my boss, and I do not want to go back to work.

✗ I do not want to use my benefits because I do not need them since I still have money in the bank.

EXPIRATION

If you wait too long, the time will expire for you to receive your check that you were perfectly qualified to get.

If you call the EDD two years later, they will say that you are not qualified for benefits because you waited too long, and therefore you are not qualified to receive any money.

PLAN B

I really hope that you have found another job by now.

If not, and you do not have any benefits, or you have used all of your unemployment benefits, and you have used all of your savings or 401(k) money, you will need to think of another strategy.

Think about who you know? Friends can be a big help in finding jobs that may not be listed online.

✓ Do you belong to any community groups?

✓ Do you attend a church or other religious institution?

✓ Who do you know at the park or in your neighborhood?

PLAN C

I go back to asking, What do you know how to do?

A part-time job is never a full-time job, but it gets money in the house to buy food, clothes, and so on.

I know many people who have three part-time jobs, and they get by. A part-time job will never be like a full-time job.

Consider taking a part-time job that will enhance your resume and maybe add new skills.

Always do your best, sometimes a part-time job can turn into a full-time position.

CONCLUSION

In my life, I have been in many different situations.

Sometimes I worked full time, and other times I worked part time. Sometimes I worked on a temporary basis, either temporary full time or temporary part time, or on a seasonal basis for Christmas or Easter.

Sometimes I worked different hours of the early morning: first shift or second shift or the night shift until midnight. There are many shifts you can take. And there are Saturday and Sunday (weekend) shifts only.

Many years I worked data entry jobs or in an office. At times I worked in stores doing retail jobs or as a cashier. Sometimes I worked taking care of children as a babysitter, and sometimes I took care of adults. I cleaned homes and took care of adult prepared food for them, and washed their clothes, sheets, tow tablecloths, and so on.

CPSIA information can be obtained
t www.ICGtesting.com
inted in the USA
HW061107060120
696BV00010B/531/P